LIFE'S
DUSTY
ROADS

May the dusty roads
in your life be full
of blessings.

Love,
Joe + Karen.

LIFE'S DUSTY ROADS

Karen Cerio

TATE PUBLISHING
AND ENTERPRISES, LLC

Published by Tate Publishing & Enterprises, LLC

127 E. Trade Center Terrace | Mustang, Oklahoma 73064 USA
1.888.361.9473 | www.tatepublishing.com

Tate Publishing is committed to excellence in the publishing industry. The company reflects the philosophy established by the founders, based on Psalm 68:11,

"The Lord gave the word and great was the company of those who published it."

Book design copyright © 2012 by Tate Publishing, LLC. All rights reserved.
Cover design by Blake Brasor
Interior design by William Lopez

Published in the United States of America

ISBN: 978-1-62024-733-4
1. Poetry / Subjects & Themes / Inspirational & Religious
2. Poetry / General
12.08.24

Dedication

For all of the survivors in this world that have chosen to live life to the fullest, and when handed lemons, they make lemonade, lemon meringue pie, and then proceed to plant the seeds.

Acknowledgments

I am praising the Lord. I thank our Lord Jesus for allowing these words to flow into my mind and out my fingers to write something that just might make a difference to someone out there, and thank You for putting my family, friends, and Tate Publishing into my world. I am grateful.

I thank my daughter for putting on her teacher's hat to help me, along with all of the members of my family and friends that for years have had to put up with me sending poems that they not only read but responded to with encouraging words and support. I thank the love of my life, my husband, Joe, for supporting me financially, spiritually, and emotionally, through thick and thin.

I thank all of the staff at Tate Publishing for thinking that my poetry had potential and for all of their help and support.

Table of Contents

Faith and Inspiration

Inspiration is entirely different
for most people that I know.

What Were You Thinking?

What were You thinking, I asked the Lord,

when You gave me a brain and a voice?

Nothing is easy in life, You said,

as You gave me a choice.

What were You thinking, I asked the Lord,

when You blessed me as

I fell on my knees to pray?

Nothing is easy in life, You said,

as You showed me the way.

What were You thinking, I asked the Lord,

when You allowed all these doubts in my mind?

Nothing is easy in life, You said,

as You answered me so kind.

What were you thinking, I asked the Lord,

when You broke my heart with a heavy

load of pain?

Nothing is easy in life, You said,

as You lifted me to a higher plain.

What were You thinking, I asked the Lord,

when You allowed such terrible burdens for me to see?

Nothing is easy in life, You said,

till you learn to trust in Me.

You are the Lord

I am a seeker

You are all power

I am weaker

I lift up my life to you.

Never Alone

God came to see me in a dream last night.

He said, My child, I love you with all of My might,

or I would not have sent My only Son

to live and to die for you and everyone.

Now child, I have something serious to say.

Listen to Me, do not waste an hour or a day

worrying yourself about your dearly departed.

They are with Me, and their life has just started.

When the time is right, you'll be together again.

With Me, you'll live too, it's a matter of when.

For now, My child,

you have angels at your side

to help you, protect you, and be your guide.

I know that your loved ones you'll miss forever.

But remember, child, you'll be alone never.

We'll send you messages in multiple ways.

Pay attention and they will brighten your days.

The pain will lessen, and may never cease,

but you will find comfort and inner peace.

Sit still, My child, and feel the great I Am,

as I hold you in My arms, My dear little lamb.

Inspiration

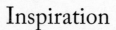

Inspiration is entirely different

for most people that I know.

For some it is high Rocky Mountains

with green valleys way below.

Others, it is warm, sandy beaches

where the soft breezes blow,

or a brilliant, beautiful sunset,

with storm clouds hanging low.

They are equally inspirational,

with many different seeds to sow,

depending upon who is looking,

and their current inner glow.

For some it is the signs of the end,

Others, God's designs to show

beginnings of peace and love

to all that take time to go

into the feelings of their heart

where the real inspirations flow.

Gift

With the gift given me by the Lord above,

most days my writing is tempered with love,

and the days it is filled with hate and fear,

are the days I know that Satan is near.

Those are the days on my knees I pray,

Lord and Savior, keep old Satan away,

help me resist all of Satan's charm,

guide me and keep me from all harm.

Grant me peace in life's churning sea.

Dear Lord Jesus, have mercy on me.

Lighthouse

He is the lighthouse on the rocky shores of life.

His beacon shines forever to guide us

through all strife.

He is there to comfort, and terror can only succeed,

where fear and disbelief follow a path

He does not lead.

The world is in big trouble with not enough

on their knees.

Many ignore the light from Him that surely

hold the keys

to a life full, rich, and happy away from hell's fiery door,

if we only pay attention

and the light do not ignore.

He has sent us many warnings to stop

the way we sin.

We are lucky He is forgiving

as we near the very end.

Floating on the seas of life,

approaching the rocky shore,

His beacon from the lighthouse

shines forevermore.

Say No

When you wake up in the morning

and just can't seem to smile,

it's the devil knocking on your door.

Say no in the name of Jesus.

When you're tempted to use

drugs or booze or take His name in vain,

it's the devil knocking on your door.

Say no in the name of Jesus.

When you gossip to a friend

trying to spread the news,

it's the devil knocking on your door.

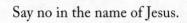

Say no in the name of Jesus.

When you question our Lord's love

and doubts creep into your heart,

it's the devil knocking on the door.

Say no in the name of Jesus.

Our Lord is good and kind and would never

put bad thoughts in your mind.

It's the devil knocking on your door.

Say no in the name of Jesus.

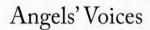

Angels' Voices

Those that have gone before us

have joined God's angelic chorus,

and with beautiful voices raised,

His name is adoringly praised.

He made all the earth and man,

all the animals, sea, and sand.

Then for every girl and boy

made a garden for them to enjoy.

The glory of God is proclaimed,

singing about His wondrous fame.

Angelic voices filled with elation

celebrate His wondrous creation

and the blessings He provides

as He stays by our sides.

Believe

Many women in the name of their rights

have against God's word put up fights.

Even Eve, with paradise in her sights,

went against God and caused our plights.

Roe vs. Wade, what happened there?

We kill babies God put in our care.

It reminds me of the woman O'Hare.

Now in our schools, there is no prayer.

∽∾

What is it with women and Satan's sword

that causes them to spurn our Lord?

Their souls with Satan they have gored,

in spite of the love, on them, God has poured.

I am not a chauvinist, men are as bad.

Satan's hooks are in more than one lad.

It's the devil's work this world gone mad.

The Lord looking down can only be sad.

If people knew how loving He can be,

it would not take long for all to see,

that babies are people like you and me.

For all our lives Jesus paid the fee.

God sent our Savior from heaven above,

to die for our sins, out of love.

He died freely, did not need a shove,

His peace He left us, with the mourning dove.

So if you believe in His resurrection,

ask forgiveness with deep reflection.

He'll give it to you with no correction,

and shower you with His affection...

I Pray

Our Lord Jesus is above all else

family, friends, and even ourselves.

I am asking, do you know the Lord?

Knowing Him brings our heavenly reward.

He is number one above all things.

Peace, love, and joy, He truly brings.

On my knees right now, I sincerely pray

that you will ask Him into your life to stay,

that His glory and grace will be with you

in all things that you think, say, and do.

Amen.

Unfinished Thought

Oh to have been there when Jesus

walked among men,

to follow Him, and listen,

and maybe touch His hem.

Perhaps a disciple of His, I could have been,

watching in awe as He cast out all sin.

Would I have believed, or rejected like others,

yelled, "crucify Him" or comforted His Mother...

It is still a decision we all have to make,

a decision that will determine our fate.

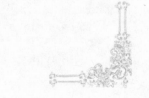

Depression

Depression sets in, I cannot think.

My mind has come close to the brink.

My heart has arrived at a ledge,

taking my body to the edge

of a cliff to a deep, dark abyss.

I refuse to go over the precipice.

My world is spinning, so I did not see

that God has something planned for me.

He'll make the plan, I must follow through

and complete all that He wants me to.

I think that I will stick around.

Keep my feet firmly on the ground,

so I can do what God thinks I should,

stay here on earth and do some good.

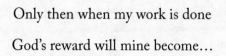

Only then when my work is done

God's reward will mine become…

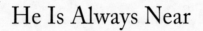

He Is Always Near

Walk like Jesus is by your side,

talk like He is right here.

Act like Jesus is by your side,

because He is always near.

When making your many life's choices,

don't forget to think about Him.

Wrong roads and confused voices

can ensure your failure with them.

You are free to do the right things,

God gave you a will of your own.

Peace and joy your life brings

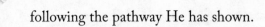

following the pathway He has shown.

Raise your voice in praise of His name

Thank Him for all you hold dear

Hold Him gently as He does the same

so you'll have no need for fear.

Walk like Jesus is by your side,

talk like He is right here.

Act like Jesus is by your side

because He is always near.

Make a Difference

Why am I here, I ask myself,

attempting to reach an upper shelf

of my mind into my very soul

to contemplate and see my life's goal?

What do You see, I ask in my mind.

My reason for living, I'm trying to find.

I have been told that You have a plan.

Lord, I'd really like to understand

what it is that You want me to do

before I can happily come to see You.

Yes, You gave me a specific guide

on how to live and I cannot hide

behind my own apathy and disbelief

just waiting for an emotional relief.

Living and dying go hand in hand

tied together with Your golden band.

I continue to help determine how both will be

with the many choices You've given to me.

I must make a difference, my thoughts repeat.

You'll take me when Your plan is complete.

So I'll continue to muddle through,

try my best to do what You want me to

and someday the answer I will see

in Your time and when You take me.

Me and the Lord

Sunday morning, not a cloud in the sky,

not in church, I'll tell you why.

Make no mistake, I love the Lord,

He and I are of one accord.

I don't always go to a building to pray.

I talk to Jesus each and every day,

in the shower, in the kitchen, the hall,

indoors, outdoors, even the mall.

He knows I love Him more than life itself,

as He loves me and gave of Himself.

He is in my heart, my mind, and by my side.

He's given me angels to be my guide,

to love generously, to deeply care,

to help me to see Him everywhere.

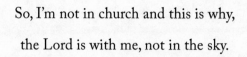

So, I'm not in church and this is why,

the Lord is with me, not in the sky.

Inside

Referred to as our Lord in heaven above

He is here inside us with all of His love.

Here when we smile at a child at play,

He stays with us all each and every day.

Although He is also in the clouds in the sky,

in mountains, valleys, and streams rushing by,

He is here inside us and our fellow man,

reaching out to all a helping hand.

So in your search for the Lord above,

look inside the heart full of love.

You will find not only peace and compassion,

but Jesus Himself our only salvation.

Trust In Him

Trust is earned, as is respect.

Love and forgiveness are given direct,

by God to you and me, so we will care

about mankind and all will share.

What good is having anything,

if in your heart you do not bring

it along wherever you may go,

to give to others and to show

God, He did not waste His time,

showing us His great design?

His Son is shining in our hearts,

though the world outside is very dark.

No matter what, we are not afraid.

We know that we can make the grade,

but cannot go very far on our own.

We need the path the Lord has shown,

of faith, forgiveness, respect, and trust

that beyond the end, He'll still love us.

His Plan

It is said things happen for a reason,

all things have a time and a season.

When it happens, we may not understand.

Might even question the use of God's hand,

but the end result is always the same,

for the good of those, who praise His name.

Most of us stop and question why,

as we kneel in prayer and gaze at the sky.

Answers are usually not revealed.

We must live the life that God does deal,

and only have to put it all in His hands.

"Believe in Me" rings out through the lands.

Biblical words sent by Him to comfort us all,

to get us to stop and heed His loving call,

to let go of all of the worldly things,

trust in Him and the plan that He brings.

Belief, faith, trust, grace, and hope,

He gives to all helping us to cope,

with all things in their time and season,

especially when we cannot see the reason.

Love and Kindness

You sneeze, and a stranger says bless you.

I am wondering, what is it that you do?

Do you remember Ms. Manner's rule book?

Acknowledge it with a smile or a kind look,

and then leave with a simple thank you,

or say thank you and God bless you too?

Do you spread His kindness all around

and share His love that you have found

or get embarrassed and maybe hesitate

to confirm God's love before it's too late,

and you let the stranger that blesses you

leave without a "God bless you too"?

Jesus's disciples denied knowledge of Him,

and we are no different than any of them.

They were just people and regular kind of men

that were there when His journey did begin.

They chose to show their faith and follow,

at times even they were embarrassed and hollow.

Does the Lord expect more from us than them?

He does want us to not be followers of men,

but to walk in His path and plant the seed

so others will know and recognize their need

to share His love that they also have found

and spread His love and kindness all around.

Reward

What do you want for a heavenly reward?

Is it enough to be with the Lord?

On earth we pray and ask for things,

money and stuff that money brings.

Of course we ask for health and love,

peace carried by a mourning dove,

also patience and wisdom and strength

and courage to help us to go the length.

So God gives us one test after another

developing those things one after the other,

helping to meet the trials of everyday living

thankful that our God is so forgiving.

Because it is so easy for us to stray,

hard making right choices every day.

From the beginning till our time is done

choices are made by each and every one.

They can make Him bow His head and say

I must carry them yet another day,

as He promised us to leave us never

and walk with us and be there forever,

so He continues to stay by our sides.

Give Him thanks for all that He provides,

for all of us on this earthly place

till we can gaze into His loving face,

knowing it is enough to be with the Lord,

realizing He is our ultimate heavenly reward.

Let Go

Fear again raises its ugly face,

taking me to an unwanted place,

where things happen in my mind.

Not things of the really good kind,

more like stuff that bumps in the night,

imaginary things so I turn on the light

'cause I had the heebie jeebies scared out of me,

and I need the light so that I can see

the fear is in my head not close to real,

with the imaginary I think I can deal.

Then calmly I can turn out the light,

and say a prayer to eliminate the fright.

Thanking God's angels for being there

right on my pillow touching my hair,

giving me comfort and doing their best

to calm my fears and help me to rest.

This fear was a fear of what's to be,

a future not knowing what I will see.

Once again the feeling was peacefully odd,

as I made the choice to let go and let God.

Developing peace as I trust Him more,

with no concern for what He has in store.

On His amazing grace, my soul will feed

and help me to follow His glorious lead,

asking Him to take over my life's plans

as I place my all in His powerful hands.

Innocent

Watch a two year old run through the park.

Their only fear could be one of the dark,

but for now they are following an inside spark.

You will remember, it will leave a mark.

As the energy shines in their happy face,

(full of God's love and unending grace)

it sends them bouncing all over the place,

sometimes invading your personal space.

This child could teach us a thing or two

about life and love and the right thing to do.

They are still innocent unlike me and you.

They have no prejudice; no judgments ensue.

Their love of life and exuberant cheers

help us stay young and turn back the years,

so we no longer feel our pent-up fears.

We smile, and for a minute, there are no tears.

If we could just see things through their eyes,

we would be happy and finally realize

all of life should be treated like the prize

that God intended when He blessed our lives.

From the Heart

Wonderful memories and beautiful places
love and laughter and smiling faces…

For Joey

I was young once, and life was fun.

Playing on the beach in the warm sun

was a virtual dream come true

the only thing missing, of course, was you.

I had no inkling, I was a young teen

and you had not yet come into my scene.

I did not know what God had in store

until I grew up and walked out the door.

At first being on my own was a blast,

quickly I learned I should not live as fast,

or try to be like a lot of my generation,

getting high on a continual celebration.

I did not get into the druggie thing,

being high on life made my heart sing.

I knew about God and religion and such,

but really never thought about it that much.

We met, then married,

did the best we could,

raised the children like we thought we should.

We had good times, bad times, up and down,

but managed to keep our feet on the ground.

I was a lot older when I started to realize,

it was God's love that was shown in our eyes.

He put us together for

His perfect reasons

to stay on His pathway throughout life's seasons.

Age crept upon us with a surprising pace,

and when I look back at our human race,

I know now, whether together or apart,

God bound you

and I with love in our heart.

When one or both of us go to His heavenly gate,

we will gratefully obtain our eternal estate.

We

Wonderful memories and beautiful places,

love and laughter and smiling faces,

our reflections in a looking glass,

the mirror edged in antique brass,

shows that we had an amazing glow

as together our lives and love did flow.

We met and the chemistry exploded.

The conversation was shotgun-loaded

ready to discharge at one wrong move,

then suddenly, a song, a smile, a groove

and as we danced the night away,

we swayed and talked till dawn of day.

You made an attempt to close the door,

obvious about your wanting more,

but in the end common sense arrived.

It's probably why our love has survived.

As we danced, listening to the band

respect was born, not a one night stand.

We managed to keep our priorities right,

our children, our home, our goals all in sight.

Looking in the mirror edged in antique brass

we see happy reflections in the looking glass.

Love and laughter and smiling faces,

wonderful memories and beautiful places.

Sparkling Eyes

To see your eyes sparkle

with love and childlike delight

when someone you love

comes into your sight

brings such satisfaction

to the inner parts of me.

Such a beautifully

orchestrated sight to see,

better than the music

drifting on the night wind.

With the song it does sing,

copious tears could begin.

Tears of great happiness

stirring feelings of joy,

caressings that nothing

on the earth can destroy.

No sorrow or sadness

that this life can bring

can diminish satisfaction

brought by the sight

of your eyes sparkling

with love and childlike delight.

Valentine

I looked for a card saying how I felt,

a card that's words your heart would melt.

Card after card, the words weren't there,

to tell you how much I really care.

You are always there when I need you,

to hold me and help me know what to do.

We've been together over twenty-eight years,

good times, bad times, laughter, and tears.

We raised our kids and have a nice home,

and even when apart are never alone.

You are my friend, my lover, my life.

I thank the Lord that I am your wife.

I'm forever yours, you're forever mine.

I love you, my valentine

The Man

I meet him and at once was impressed,

did not notice how he was dressed.

The conversation was good, not great.

He was in a hurry, running late.

I looked through his eyes into his soul,

not at the outside, but at the whole.

Oh the things that I could see,

things every man wished he could be.

Strong yet gentle, caring, and wise,

the kind of man that no one buys.

The love of the Lord shining inside,

a love he would never try to hide.

I would be proud if he was my son.

And I wish only the best for this one

man I met for a very brief time,

and that in his life, Jesus will shine.

Karen Cerio

First Kiss

Hugs and kisses

and holding hands

Long evening strolls

listening to bands

Children laughing

waking at night

Saying the wrong thing

having a fight

Looks of passion

with hearts on fire

Kindling sparks

of heated desire

All of the love,

laughter, and tears

Shared with you

all of these years

Just look at all we

would have missed

if you and I

had not first kissed...

Quiet Times

Quiet Times

Graceful Mountains

Still Waters

Cool Breezes

Starry Skies

White Sand Beaches

Soft Music

Flickering Fire

You and I

Tears

I never knew the scars were so deep.

I never knew it could still make me weep.

The healing must have been very thin,

covering the hurt that was within.

It didn't take much to open the thing.

No blood, but many tears it did bring.

Pain in a heart that was already cracked,

actually broken, when I think back

I do not know if this one will heal.

I have lost all sensation to feel.

The love that I thought was forever

was washed away down a river

of tears.

Always and Forever

Acknowledging many years well spent,

wondering where the heck they went.

Looking back time just seemed to fly

gone faster than the blink of an eye.

I think of all of the things we did.

We met when I was just a kid,

at least I was young, you were older,

me naïve, you were much bolder.

I smile when I think of good times past

and even the bad times went by too fast.

We were two bodies that were of one mind.

Today, it is called soul mate, one of a kind.

Sharing love and laughter and tears,

we built a good life over many years.

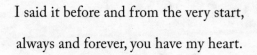

I said it before and from the very start,

always and forever, you have my heart.

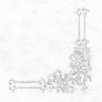

Good-bye

Good-bye

Why

You Know

Just Go

You did it many times before

Sorry doesn't get it anymore

Just Go

You Know

Why

Good-bye

Celebrations of Life

On the outside for the world to see
how beautiful life's garden can really be

Song of Celebration

Gatherings with prayerful meals,

amazing how special it all feels.

Colored eggs, sweet potatoes and ham,

Easter celebrations for the great I Am

showing faith and belief that He is alive

and with Him someday we will abide.

He paid the price for you and me

and His sacrifice has set us all free.

Then He arose on the third day

and as promised has not gone away.

He is here in our heart and our mind,

giving eternal hope to all of mankind.

I bow my head, my heart full of praise

knowing that He has blessed my days.

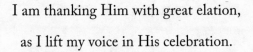

I am thanking Him with great elation,

as I lift my voice in His celebration.

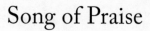

Song of Praise

Songs of His Praise have been sung

since the earth was very young.

Glorious sounds of adoration

lifting Him up in exaltation.

Comfort of spirit, peace of mind,

a serenity that we all can find

with the acceptance of His grace,

and His warm, loving embrace.

For His Word given as our guide

and for all that He does provide,

songs of thanksgiving we now sing

to the glory of Christ our King.

The Best Gift

Christmas morning we all awake

hoping Saint Nicholas wasn't late.

Few of us ever stop and remember

to thank God for this December.

We think only of gifts under the tree

and not the Son given to you and me,

to shed His blood and make amends

to die on the cross for our sins.

The best gift we will ever receive

was sent from God one December Eve.

So, when you wake this Christmas morn,

think of Jesus and why He was born.

Thank the Lord in heaven above

for the gift of His eternal love.

Enjoy Today

Life is short is what they say.

Tomorrow is a brand-new day.

Not knowing what it will bring,

thank the Lord for everything.

Enjoy today for what it is.

Listen to the song of a bird.

It's a message without a word.

A song of life and love and joy,

telling every girl and boy to

enjoy today for what it is.

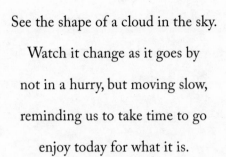

See the shape of a cloud in the sky.

Watch it change as it goes by

not in a hurry, but moving slow,

reminding us to take time to go

enjoy today for what it is.

Taste the smells of dinner cooking,

heavenly scents, to send us looking

for comfort food from a warm oven

with cozy feelings of family lovin'.

Enjoy today for what it is.

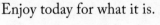

Ponder the wonders of this earth,

snow drifting slowly, a new baby's birth.

A Christ Child sent to show the way,

to have peace and joy come what may.

Enjoy today for what it is.

Still

Sit still and quietly,

feel the great I Am.

As the world awakens

softly like a newborn lamb,

the sun is shining down

on Mother Nature's face.

Amazing God's creatures

roaming a wondrous place.

Antelope, squirrels,

majestic big horn sheep,

mountain lion, kit fox,

all no longer asleep.

Red rock formations

reaching up to the sky,

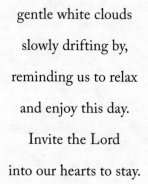

gentle white clouds

slowly drifting by,

reminding us to relax

and enjoy this day.

Invite the Lord

into our hearts to stay.

Take Time

"Go lightly," whispered the breeze,

as it rustled leaves on the trees.

"Take time for the gifts of the Lord."

"Listen quietly," said the atmosphere,

as it filled the lungs of a trembling deer.

"Take time for the gifts of the Lord."

"Step softly," murmured the air,

as it moved gently through her hair.

"Take time for the gifts of the Lord."

"Stop briefly," roared the gale,

as it whipped down mountain and dale.

"Take time for the gifts of the Lord."

"Pray deeply," thundered the heavens,

reminding us what we have been given.

"Take time for the gifts of the Lord..."

Free

Butterfly, butterfly, flitting around,

you very rarely touch the ground.

Your colors are so clear and bright.

You are shining beauty in the sunlight.

Beautiful butterfly, you fly so free.

Not a care in the world for people to see.

You fly 'round bushes from flower to flower

not knowing that you have a wonderful power,

to pollinate the earth and help things grow

to sow seeds of life, 'cause God made it so.

Life's Garden

My beautiful garden, no matter the care,

sometimes weeds grow here and there.

Now, I can choose to ignore the weeds,

let it grow and grow and scatter its seeds

until it entirely takes over my garden.

But, no, I won't, I beg your pardon.

I will pull the weeds for the compost pile

and cause my beautiful garden to smile.

Somehow I think this is similar to living.

The weeds of life will keep on giving

unless we choose to throw them out,

do not allow them to make us pout.

Toss them in life's compost heaps

allowing us to live and take giant leaps

toward the inner smile of our own,

actually spreading it so that it is shown

on the outside for the world to see

how beautiful life's garden can really be.

Dusty Roads

Dusty roads, I'm traveling down,

dusty roads, from town to town.

Headed west on old Route Sixty-Six,

listening to a country mix,

waving at truckers as they go by,

glad I'm driving and did not fly.

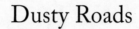

Been clear across the great USA

so many times that I know the way.

Been to Gramp's Camp in the midst of Maine,

it's on a small pond of no real fame.

I've seen the New York City skyline,

looked at a Pennsylvania coal mine,

seen autumn leaves on the Mohawk trail,

and rode the Frisco underground rail.

I worked in the Kansas farmlands,

helped feed Nebraska harvest hands,

and sang to cattle under a big blue sky.

I found the answer and now know why

this country of ours is really the best,

with people and parks from east to west.

Now, I'm finding my way back home,

getting too old and too tired to roam.

∽

Headed west on old Route Sixty-Six,

listening to a country mix,

waving at truckers as they go by,

glad I'm driving and did not fly.

Dusty roads, I'm traveling down,

dusty roads, I'm homeward bound.

New Year

Christmas has come and gone.

Snow is still covering the lawn.

Santa is back home in his bed,

with sugar plums in his head.

And the New Year is upon us.

The kids are in having a snack.

Broken toys already taken back,

batteries dead and none around,

trains and games run aground.

And the New Year is upon us.

Mom and Dad are thinking about a nap.

He's no longer wearing the cap,

contemplating all of this last year,

full of laughter and an occasional tear.

And the New Year is upon us.

Family, friends, love that will last,

come to mind thinking of the past.

Resolutions not entirely made yet,

party planning and streamers to get.

And the New Year is upon us.

Looking to a year of good will,

of peace and joy and love to fill

our lives with awesome good cheer,

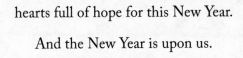

hearts full of hope for this New Year.

And the New Year is upon us.

Home and Hearth

Parents and home, love and laughter,
thoughts roam, forever after
to Kansas.

Prayer

I stood and watched the car pull away

and closed my eyes and began to pray.

Dear Lord Jesus, help them on their way,

keep them safe, happy, and healthy every day.

Please enter their hearts, always to abide.

Gently hold them and be their guide.

Your love and grace do not hide,

as they travel with You by their side.

For no matter, age or daughter, son or friend,

Your love is the beginning and not the end.

All broken lives, You will surely mend,

as their walk with You they truly begin.

May they follow Your footsteps all of the way

and knock on Your door some long, distant day,

knowing that You will never turn them away.

In this I thank You as I stand and pray.

Dad

Once a Marine, always a Marine

is what my daddy said.

Honor, country, family, and God,

were things he put in my head.

Honesty, integrity, and loyalty,

respect for property and life,

were only a few of the many things

taught by the way he lived his life.

He was of German descent,

is what a lot of people would say.

But, Dad would tell you himself,

he was an American all the way.

Born and raised in Kansas,

with a Bible at home on the stand,

he worked from sunrise to sunset

no doubt he was a real man.

He chose the Marines in wartime.

He fought as hard as he lived.

He sent his check to his momma,

to help with the farm and the kids.

He returned, he said, not a hero,

and would not talk about the war.

He concentrated on living then,

getting back to things from before.

I really do miss my dad,

as he's been gone several years,

But honor, country, family, and God

still shine out through my tears.

Why

With the world full of terror, trouble, and strife

I find myself thinking more and more about life.

Why do things happen both good and bad,

things that make me both happy and sad?

Why in the world do I do what I do?

Why in the world did I ever meet you?

Then today while sitting and thinking of things,

it hit that you are the gift God did bring.

With His infinite wisdom from heaven above,

He gave me a friend, someone to love.

A friend to help me fight Satan's sword

and gently remind me to trust in the Lord.

Home

Flat lands, oceans of wheat,

harvest hands, fields all neat

friendly folks, warm smiles,

country jokes, at-home styles,

family fun, 4th of July,

summer sun, stars in the sky,

county fair, carnival lights,

first-place mare, dances at night,

drive-in features, friends for life,

old teachers, help in strife,

tornado warnings, siren blasts,

Sunday morning, faith that lasts,

skies of blue, thunder clouds,

grass with dew, funeral shrouds,

simple food, gathering eggs,

city dude, bowed legs,

handshake deals, respect of man,

prayerful kneels, God and land,

parents and home, love and laughter,

thoughts roam, forever after

to Kansas.

A Friend

A friend died a few years ago.

I wasn't in town, I didn't know.

She had cancer, how she fought,

tried to survive, loved life a lot.

I visited her on most days.

She touched me in many ways.

Then, in December on the 21st day,

I hopped a plane and flew away.

I saw her smile the day before.

She said, "I'm ready, so is the Lord,"

but she'd wait till I returned.

She died the 22nd, I later learned.

I saw her face in my dream,

she was peaceful and serene.

She said, "No worry, I've gone away.

I've gone home with Jesus to stay."

Fly Away

Fly away, fly away you are free,

to be on your own away from me.

You are an adult now.

You have to see

the big world outside as it should be.

I will say a prayer on bended knee

for the Lord to smile

always on thee,

to make you happy,

you deserve to be,

keep you safe without me.

Out of the nest, my chickadee,

just fly away, fly away

you are free.

Empty Nest

Lord have mercy, it was hard to accept

my baby left home, oh how I wept.

For days and days, my eyes filled with tears.

"Empty nest syndrome," they call these years.

When the others left it wasn't as bad.

I love them too and was very sad,

but when they left, I still felt the need

of the one still home, the last of our seed.

I began to think I was spinning a wheel,

making no progress with how I feel.

I can take pain of the physical kind

better than the pain of heart and mind,

that mothers have to go through,

Watching the things their children do.

As they work their way through this life,

making mistakes that can hurt like a knife.

Some succeeding and soaring to the sky,

with not a clue about the how and the why.

The Lord allows them to make the choice

and pick Him or not with a strong voice.

It is not habit, because I really do care,

all of these years with them I share.

Now they're all grown and on their own,

with seeds of their life that they have sown.

Now the empty nest feels pretty good

and so do I, as God knew I would.

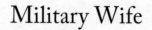

Military Wife

Hard is the life of the military wife

whose man is overseas.

Damned if she does and damned if she don't,

no one she can appease.

She works, no play, only time to pray

frequently on her knees.

She's asking the Lord to help her please.

Mom

Such amazing beauty and thing of delight

is the dragonfly in the midst of flight.

They were for my mom a favorite thing

and still today, they make my heart sing

with memories of love and laughter

that will remain with me forever after.

A gentle reminder that I am not alone,

she would never leave me all on my own.

Even though God took her to live with Him,

her message of love and life will never dim.

She forever cares and watches over me,

ensuring that life's beauty I continue to see.

Through the dragonfly or the mourning dove,

she daily sends messages of undying love.

Eternally sending them in the midst of flight,

such amazing beauty and things of delight.

Childhood Memories

Childhood memories spring to the front

of my train of thought.

They bring a smile and a feeling of comfort

that cannot be bought.

For as a young child, though quiet and shy,

I was loved so much.

The fiber of my life was living, laughing,

family, and such.

I, of course, had parents, siblings, cousins,

aunts, and uncles too,

The grandparents were the very best,

just between me and you.

They loved me unconditionally,

and taught without preaching.

The way that they lived

was their natural way of teaching.

I admit to an occasional dose of badness

when things were not just right.

It never lasted very long and was gone

like the flick of a light.

I learned that living life your very best

was the only way to go,

to never sit and watch the world

go by leaving you feeling low.

What good is actually getting

there if you do not enjoy the ride.

Take time to smell the roses

on the way to move the tide.

When memories of childhood days

jump into my mind,

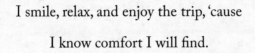

I smile, relax, and enjoy the trip, 'cause

I know comfort I will find.

To My Sister

Daughter, sister, wife, and mother,

For her life she'd trade no other.

A nicer person you'll not find,

As in her heart she is very kind.

I know her well, as she is my sister.

We are miles apart, and I really miss her.

Although we'll always live far apart,

She is forever here, in my heart.

To you, my sister, I send my love,

and prayers for blessings from our Lord above.

Woman

She is awake and up at six

to have her early coffee fix.

To do her exercise routine,

(it is really not too obscene),

then out onto the deck her world

she does inspect.

She starts to pull the weeds

and finishes planting seeds,

checks and fixes the garden wall.

The phone rings, she takes a call,

makes a promise to a friend

she'll honor it until the end,

then prepares and stores many meals

and jumps behind the wheel,

to go see family and hug a child.

At the store she'll go slightly wild.

Back home to fix the bathroom sink,

sit a minute to try to think.

Yes, she thinks she did have lunch,

and she responded on a hunch

to a deal with both of the banks,

even remembered to say thanks.

She did all that she intended to,

there is little more she'll need to do.

Check the doors, the computer, head to bed,

and say prayers before laying down her head,

to say good night, sleep tight,

don't let the bed bugs bite…

BFF

Best friends forever,

a term overused and abused.

We know many people,

few friends do we choose.

Friends are there for us

in spite of our faults.

They see them yet know

inside our minds' vaults.

We're not always tactful

and sometimes rude.

We're occasionally dull

and act like a prude.

They've seen us cry

at the drop of a hat.

Understand when we buy

or gripe cause we're fat.

Real friends are forever

in life's scheme of things,

laughter, joy, and comfort

their friendship brings.

Angels

I met an angel at the park one day,

saw her helping a child at play.

Lo and behold there was another one,

it seems their work is never done.

I continued to look all around

for these angels that are earthbound.

I began to see them everywhere,

spreading love and showing they care.

Helping a senior cross a busy street,

standing so someone can have their seat,

reading for a class to have a head start,

sharing a hug to heal a hurting heart,

listening to a soul filled with pain,

giving themselves with no personal gain,

serving food to a homeless man,

gladly contributing a helping hand.

I looked closer at these angels of men.

I saw they are a neighbor and a friend,

smiling, laughing, and sharing their love,

helping God's angels sent from above.

So check your mirror, what do you see?

I see that you are an angel sent to me.

Thank you.

Grandchildren

A daughter, two sons, a total of three,

have given eight grandchildren to me.

They have a special place in my heart,

always did from the very start

of life when they were born,

sunshine to brighten up the morn.

All of them are like bread and honey,

sweet and fun and very sunny.

They have great big smiles of cheer,

with loving hugs that are so dear.

I do not see them often enough,

on heart and mind that is really tough.

But everyone has lives to live,

and gives everything they have to give.

So this ancient, decrepit, wrinkled old fart

holds them in a special place in her heart.

I truly love them, each and every one,

and will even after my life is done.

Miracle

I once was a child full of love and laughter

living in my dream world of forever after.

I had no concept of the things that would be,

both happy and sad that would happen to me.

I became a young lady spreading my wings,

full of love and dreams of magnificent things.

Things I thought I would be and have and do.

Young enough there was not yet a thought of you.

Old enough to realize life was going to be hard,

more complicated than a mere flip of a card.

Friends and family floating out of my sight,

things not in my control giving me fright.

Then came adulthood settling in with strength,

I was happy knowing I could go the length,

achieving the things of my younger dreams,

but what's important had changed, or so it seems.

Suddenly I am old. My memory beginning to fail,

even my dreams have become distant and frail.

I am no longer looking at what my life brings,

but watching you begin spreading your wings,

excited for all the things you are going to see.

Praying you will feel as loved and happy as me.

Discovering your dream world of forever after,

my miracle grandchild full of love and laughter.

Gifts of Love

As I look out across wide open spaces,

I wonder at God making all of these places.

Giving mankind this breathtaking view,

all of these great things to see and to do.

Is it a bluff, butte, mesa, or plateau?

What do I call it? I really don't know.

The dictionary was not much help.

It kept referring to them all up on a shelf

of land that rises from the earth into the sky.

The English language can't help to specify

what to call these gifts from our Lord above.

Guess I will call them gifts of love.

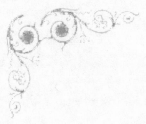

Life's Journey

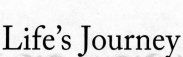

It is what it is, nature's chorus knows,
just do your best then on life goes.

Life

Thinking of life could crush the average man,

if the Lord wasn't there to help him stand.

There's calls to make and bills to pay,

kids to raise and show the way,

cuts and bruises and hearts to heal,

production and sales to wheel and deal.

Cars break down, and taxes go up.

Nicotine is cancer if a rat drinks a cup.

With attorneys to hassle, depositions to give,

it can make you wonder, why do we live?

Thinking of life could crush

the average man,

if the Lord wasn't there

to help him stand.

Follow

Life goes on, we do our best

until determined it's time to rest.

Troubles are faced and defeated.

Happiness abounds with deeply seeded

hope and love living in our hearts,

when from His path we do not part.

Our lives held gently in His hands,

He sends His blessings throughout the lands.

It is when we choose not to follow,

in guilt and sadness, we will wallow.

Thieves will steal, murderers will kill,

but only when they ignore His will.

Always His love and forgiveness abound.

Faith and prayer and all souls can be found.

Once again our lives held in His hands,

as He blesses us all throughout the lands.

Root of All Evil

The root of all evil, what could it be,

alcohol, drugs, promiscuity,

greed, power, jealousy,

war, hunger, poverty,

nuclear weapons, or idolatry.

The root of all evil, I know what it is,

the rejection of Jesus and all that is His.

A Child's Eye

Remember seeing things through a child's eye.

Forever wondering at the how and why

the stars twinkle up in a dark, dark sky,

or maybe why clouds gently float by

and how birds and planes can actually fly

as technology happens we say, oh my,

or why everything eventually has to die.

Evolution or Creation, which do we buy,

asking is science a truth or theoretical lie?

It causes God to breathe a heavy sigh.

He gave us the knowledge and desire to try

and always wonder at the how and the why,

to remember seeing things through a child's eye.

Going Upstream

Life's disappointments are hard to swallow

especially when we seem to wallow

in the despair of sometimes heavy grief.

We try and try to make it brief,

by getting ourselves to go upstream,

but making progress feels like a dream

until one day we suddenly awaken

and look back at the trail we have taken

with all of its various twists and turns.

It took some time, but we did learn

to let go and move on past the pain

so that now we begin to live life again.

God gave us our spirit forever after,

no excuse needed for fun and laughter.

Happiness, we do not have to steal,

it is a gift from God and very real.

He truly expects us to not waste living,

to go the length and to keep on giving

from every fiber of our very existence,

to destroy despair with all our resistance

and then build upon all that we know

by taking time to help others and show

them how we managed to get upstream

so they too can realize their dream.

To lift up others and give them help

is to lift up ourselves to a higher shelf.

Who's There?

I looked in the mirror and what did I see,

a little old lady looking back at me.

Someone was there I did not know,

gray hair and wrinkles, she did show.

Something had happened to her backside.

It was at least two axe handles wide.

What I was seeing could not be real.

Impossible, but it's me, I began to feel.

I know on the inside I'm just twenty-one,

young and thin and filled with fun.

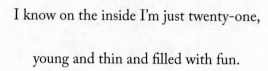

This could not have happened overnight.

It must be the angle of the light.

This could not have happened overnight.

I looked in the mirror and what did I see,

A little old lady, and it was me...

I Forget

Dementia is the name.

Forgetting is the game.

It is my turn today,

but I do not want to play,

this game that I cannot win.

Frustration quickly sets in

as I try to remember

closer than some December.

Names and dates are used,

I get them all confused.

I am told that my brain

is like an abandoned train,

on a side track, just sitting there,

dreaming and going nowhere.

Really I do not have a clue

about what to say or what to do

to actually play this game

that I can't remember its name.

It Is What It Is

A baby bird fell from its nest.

We tried to save it, we did our best.

But as is the natural order of things,

it is no more, but the mom still sings.

It is what it is, nature's chorus knows,

just do your best, then on life goes.

A flower grows and makes you smile.

Its beauty will last a very short while,

and eventually it will go away.

God did not send it here to stay.

It is what it is, nature's chorus knows,

just do your best, then on life goes.

A spider works hard to trap a fly.

One gust of wind, and it is good-bye

and she must build the web again

Against nature's order, she cannot defend.

It is what it is, nature's chorus knows

just do your best, then on life goes.

We can complain and moan and groan,

but will not change a thing on our own.

The moral of the story, I relate to the ant,

never give up, never say that you can't.

It is what it is, nature's chorus knows

just do your best, then on life goes.

When the circle of life is complete,

God will carry us home, there will be no defeat.

Trust the natural order of things to prevail,

and in God's hands, our spirits will sail.

It is what it is, nature's chorus knows

just do your best, then on life goes.

Life's Memories

My mind is no longer what it used to be

I forget and get confused so easily.

Some say it is nothing more than age,

or not focusing, like getting lost on a page

of a book that I am trying to read,

others have doubts and they planted the seed.

Could it be a form of dementia spreading?

Will I no longer know where I am heading,

or what to call this, this thing-a-ma-bob?

(You know, it makes my head throb.)

Will I forget all the love and laughter,

my family, my home, and what comes after?

Right this minute I know, and I am afraid,

this crazy disease will continue to pervade

and I will not be me, myself anymore,

I will turn the corner and close my mind's door.

Then all of life's memories will fade away.

I'll be in that new world forever to stay.

Mother's Plea

Long ago the war to end all wars was fought.

We won that one, and everyone cheered a lot.

Then came the big one, to end all war,

when over they said there'd be no more.

Next was Korea, it was called a conflict,

then Viet Nam, with no word that would fit.

Now we are in Saudi, will there be a fight?

Some say, "Hit them hard with all our might."

Others yell, "No, there is no reason why

for oil and money our troops should die."

Or is it freedom that sends us there,

Hussein and Iraq taking more than their share.

What do we say to the people of Kuwait?

Freedom's a dream, so suffer your fate?

Big brothers we're not,

put your dreams on the shelf.

God helps them that help themselves.

We'll get involved and only help out,

when Washington hears Iraq's shout.

When they attack our own shore,

we'll wish we helped you

a whole lot more.

God have mercy if we don't help our brother,

'cause He put us here to help each other.

So stand proud, America,

land of the free,

and pray that is how it will always be.

My husband's time in the service is done.

Now the army has both of my sons.

I pray every day

they will not have to fight.

If they do help me support their plight,

in everything that I say and do,

'cause they are fighting for me and you...

Mother's Plea Update

Well what can I say, it's two thousand ten.

We did not do what we should have back then.

They attacked our land in two thousand and one.

They killed thousands of people

before they were done.

And after all these many years have gone by

our planes are still in the air, our men still fly,

over foreign lands trying to put an end

to the devastating war that terrorists did begin.

I think the last one was called Desert Storm.

Now it's a war against terror

and it's not the norm,

'cause suicide bombs from children,

women, and men,

are used to cripple and kill

and are hard to defend.

My sons made it back; now,

my grandson is the age to fight.

Lord I pray for You

to help to make everything right.

Keep our troops safe and

bring them home now.

Put a stop to this madness.

Only You know how...Amen.

Silent Screams

America, land of the free, all hail

Mothers are now being sent to jail,

with charges of crimes against the unborn,

yet that baby could have been torn

limb from limb from its mother's womb

and thrown into a trash-filled tomb.

All in the name of rights and choice,

silent screams of an unheard voice

echoing quietly all over the earth.

God should question creation's worth.

He gave us knowledge of good and bad,

and we murder our own, how very sad.

If I was God, I wouldn't be forgiving.

I'd take my wrath out on the living.

People would think they were in hell,

until on their knees, everyone fell.

So thank the Lord that I'm not He,

Because He will forgive you and me.

Please join me now on our knees to pray,

for the Lord to forgive us all today,

for what we did or did not do,

please have mercy on me and you.

And, Lord, we entrust in your hands

our babies and children all over the lands,

to guide and care for with infinite love

till they are with you in heaven above.

Montana Man

The man from Montana, a two-fisted drinker

his brain is pickled, so he's not a thinker.

To prove he's a man, he's bossy and mean,

acts like a jerk, always causing a scene.

He's taken advantage of lots of women,

ruined their lives when their love they've given.

He can be a real charmer; he is at the start,

just long enough to steal their heart.

Then all of a sudden, true colors he'll fly.

When he's done, you'll want to die.

He'll take your house, your car, and the keys

and charge up your cards with big-time fees.

The bill collectors will try to collect,

your pockets empty, you've lost self respect

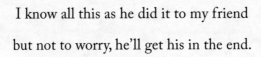

I know all this as he did it to my friend

but not to worry, he'll get his in the end.

Addict

Yes, I am an addict, I've known it for years.

Caffeine & nicotine jump-start my gears.

My addictions are legal, won't send me to jail.

I may lose my life, but I won't need bail.

You see, years ago when I was a pup,

smoking was cool, coffee to get up.

So, I started smoking in alleys with friends,

the beer & Jack Daniels' supply had no end.

I finally woke up one endless day

and threw the Jack Daniels and beer away.

I've even quit smoking, cut out nicotine,

stopped all coffee, no more caffeine.

Something always happens, excuses, I think.

So, cigarettes I smoke and coffee I drink.

"I hope God forgives me," I cry with tears,

for I am an addict, I've known it for years

Twenty years later, and coffee I still drink.

Open heart surgery made me stop and think.

So with great trepidation, I gave up nicotine,

cold turkey on cigarettes, but not the caffeine.

Slow Down

I do not Facebook, YouTube, or Twitter.

I even use snail mail, with cards that glitter.

Guess I'm old-fashioned, not of speed and excess.

Taking time to write, is my way to address.

E-mail is a good form of communication,

quicker than snail mail to its destination.

Of course I'd rather talk face-to-face,

impossible in this day of the human race.

Society dictates things move so fast.

What happened to enjoying our repast?

Sit down for a meal and actually talk,

maybe when done even take a walk.

Look a friend straight in the eye,

give them a hug, actually say good-bye.

Look around you and say a prayer,

Thanking God for what He's put there.

Let's slow it down, but not to a crawl,

before we go so fast, we all take a fall.

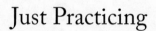

Just Practicing

Human illness comes in many forms,

some of which is outside the norms

of the medical profession's expertise.

In spite of the knowledge they did seize

from all of those years spent in school

studying the aspects inside the rule,

they treat symptoms and not the cause,

in fear of attorneys and malpractice laws,

and insist on treating everyone the same,

so they are intent on practicing the game.

Oops, there is the word that is the key,

they practice medicine on you and me.

Pity Party

Woulda, coulda, shoulda, what did they ever do

besides confuse the facts and me and you.

None of them ever, ever fixed a thing.

Guilt and mixed feelings are all that they bring

to any pity party that they choose to attend

(then they usually stay till the very end)

If is another word that belongs up there

when used in reference to a past-tense affair,

as it is something that does nothing at all

unless used planning to avoid a future appall.

So who really cares,? you shout with raised voices

this simply validates the importance of choices.

Step back and think while there is a chance,

while you still have options,

before you advance,

and can direct what you actually believe, say, or do,

that could have an effect on more than just you.

Pray for His guidance to help following His will

and that you can continue to proceed uphill

so woulda, coulda, shoulda do not cross your mind.

You found peace and happiness of His glorious kind.

No Discrimination

Equal opportunity, no discrimination,

famous in your mind or the entire nation,

rich as a king or poor as a mouse,

live in a castle or not have a house,

older than dirt or newborn kind,

black, white, or brown, you it can find.

It eats at the body, the heart, and mind,

and it can kill if it is the wrong kind.

The thought brings us to our knees in fear,

praying out loud for just one more year.

Experimental drugs take many chances.

There is no cure just remission advances.

You have a choice on what to do,

moan and groan and feel sorry for you,

or deserve your life, kick it in gear.

Live like you should, conquer the fear.

Set an example like others I know,

live, love, and laugh wherever you go.

It is your job to stand up and fight.

God will decide when to turn out the light.

Then, when it is time, you can look back and say,

Thank You, Lord, I lived and loved every day.

Words

There are several words that people hear

that make them cringe and tremble in fear.

Cancer, of course, is mostly number one,

melanoma is caused by too much sun.

In reality cancer of any type,

devastatingly lives up to its hype.

Then the term is heart attack,

with little chance of coming back.

Similar vibes when you hear "stroke"

with lasting effects that are no joke.

Death is another word of taboo

and comes at the end of the others too.

There are so many, it's impossible to list,

but I know that you get the gist.

In the middle of all words that scare,

come comforting words showing care.

Urging us to take any and all steps,

to never rely on just heavy bets,

but give our lives over to His power

to trust in Him each and every hour.

To easily ensure we will not be alone

make His loving promise our very own.

No matter what word or term we face,

we will be held in His loving embrace.

Straight

He went to jail for the third time in his young life,

and this time he left behind a child and a wife.

The first time,

the echo of the closing of the detention gate

made him shudder and swear that he would go straight.

It was not long after he was back out on the street,

while in a fit of depression,

an old friend he did meet.

The friend made a promise to help him

have some fun.

He smoked some dope,

unaware the friend had a gun.

He was pretty high when things got carried away.

Then once again

he was taken to jail for a stay.

This time when they slammed that big prison gate,

he prayed and promised that he would go straight.

And out, he managed to keep up and stay clean,

with a job, wife, and child,

he tried the family scene.

He forgot about his promise when things got rough.

He forgot about Jesus,

and he talked big and tough,

blaming the whole wide world for his state in life.

He thought they owed him,

so he stole with a knife.

The last time that they slammed that prison gate,

he prayed on his knees when he vowed to go straight.

Believe it or not,

his story proceeds in a positive light.

He has managed

to keep the Lord Jesus in his sight.

He accepted responsibility

and became a changed man.

He loves the Lord and his family

as much as anyone can.

When he passes that old friend on the street today,

he says a prayer for him too,

asking the Lord to stay

and help keep him from ever hearing

that prison gate.

He is thankful forever

because he has stayed straight…

They

Society today is obsessed, it seems,

with things and beauty and means.

If you have none of the above,

then you society does not love.

They want everyone to be the same,

talk and walk and play the game,

the way that someone said is right.

Different can certainly cause a fight.

Heaven help the man on the street,

that looks directly at those he may meet.

Lord have mercy on the local bum,

they assume that he is really dumb.

If you are black, white, or blue,

and do something unexpected of you,

they become self-righteous judges,

pushing you out with unkind nudges.

Then if in public you dare say a prayer,

they tisk with indignity, and they stare.

I continually ask, who the heck is this they

that tries to tell everyone what to do and say?

Who is it that died and made them kings,

judges, and rulers of all earthly things?

Well Jesus lives, He is my judge and my guide.

With Him by me, I do not have to hide.

I can be open for the theys to see

I love the Lord Jesus, and He loves me.

Reflections

Whenever I take an intensely long look
at the sands of the past
like an open book ...

Reflections of a Wandering Mind

We all have times when we just sit and think.

Possibly while we are having a drink

of water or coffee or beer or wine.

(If the last two, then our thinking is fine)

We let our thoughts ramble from work to home,

to shopping and dinner and friends to phone.

Thoughts of the children pop in the middle of it all,

then it's the grandkids that jump into the mall

of thoughts that wander around the brain,

going from one thought to another thought train.

What about diets from allergies,

or the many attempts we make to please?

Thoughts of world events jump

in now and then;

abortions, religion, human rights begin and end

in the reflection of a wandering mind.

Respect

Stop and ponder our specific life,

then let's dissect it with a surgical knife.

Most things are not important, after the fact,

just a particular situation makes us react.

Then, a subsequent lack of compromise

helps to build us up until we realize

some things in life are worth fighting for,

others are not, so why slam the door

on the possibility of a great conversation

with a chance to learn of a new creation

in the wake of someone else's dream,

as all people are worthy of equal esteem.

If respect is what you feel that you deserve,

give it to others without any reserve.

Fitting behavior in any relationship

verifies accountability in life's short trip

and shows the world with its microscope

that we are worthy of respect and hope.

Checking Out

Life is like going to a big grocery store.

Going through aisles you see more and more

of what is out there for you to choose,

and the only time you will really lose

is when you get in the checkout line

before you are done and it is not time.

Think about all of the things you would miss.

Should you have tried that or maybe this?

There are things out there to enrich your life,

choices that can bring happiness or strife.

You will never know what all is out there,

unless you go through every aisle with care,

and do not get in the checkout line,

until you are done and in God's time…

Nightmares

Nightmares of man have been told and retold.

Ghoulish monsters in fables of old,

dragons & witches & horrors of night,

make man tremble in fear at their sight.

From the very old to a strapping young lad,

fear sets in and can scar them bad.

Just one look and they run from life,

swearing never, ever to take a wife.

The worst of the worst of all man's dreams

is a woman with curlers and face cream.

Karen Cerio

Yesterday

My heart yearned

for what could have been,

old lessons learned

but ignored back then.

What a wasted youth,

I think today,

if I tell the truth

about yesterday.

Lessons taught

a long time ago

all for naught

as I let them flow

right on through

my then young mind.

Thoughts that grew

hidden, I could not find.

If I only knew then

what I know now,

where I have been

might've changed somehow.

What would I have done

with a life with no tragedy?

Would there have been fun?

Who would I really be?

I no longer yearn

for what could have been.

I like what I've learned

and my life now, because of then.

Decisions

All of us have decisions to make.

A lot depends on the course we take.

If we've money, it's where to invest,

if not, of course, it's what costs less.

Will it be a matter of yes or no,

or maybe, which gives us nowhere to go?

Will we jump in with both feet,

and somehow end up smelling sweet,

or land in a huge pile of goop

and run around in a frenzied loop?

Will we hesitate awhile too long,

till the opportunity is a song

of good-bye cause we're too late?

We straddled the fence and fell off the gate.

Trains and Brains

The mind must be like a train,

a long, cross-country Amtrak brain,

always rushing from here to there,

picking up passenger thoughts from the air.

Passenger thoughts that never get off,

but are kept stored up in the loft

until needed at a later time,

maybe only to complete a rhyme,

or generally (it must be the rule)

flitting around so you feel the fool.

Did I do it? I can't remember.

Is it my age or just a glimmer

of what happens with brain overload,

like a train off track and dead in the road?

Flu

My brain is foggy

My tongue is thick

My throat is froggy

I think I'm sick.

A pain in my back

An ache in my head

I should hit the sack

Or maybe be fed

Oh, God, have pity

I've so much to do

I work in the city

Have company too

House needs cleaned

The lawn needs mowed

Skirt needs seamed

Dishwasher to load

Oh, Lord, just thinking

Makes my head spin

I feel I'm sinking

So this is the end.

Computers

Computers are up then they're down,

makes your head spin round and round.

Right in the middle I lost that batch,

soon you'll find me in the booby-hatch.

Computers are great, they work so fast,

and store information that'll last and last.

When they're up, it can make work fun,

when down, cause headaches before you're done.

It makes you mad and makes you dizzy,

up and down on a day that is busy.

With a gun I could shoot the screen,

but that would be excessively mean.

And if the company sent me to jail,

everyone here would pitch in for bail.

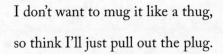

I don't want to mug it like a thug,

so think I'll just pull out the plug.

Flight

For some it's trauma, for others it's fun

while some are bored and yawn, ho hum.

Traumatic victims, knuckles white,

barely contain their screams of fright.

Fun-loving ones go with a smile

and giggle and talk mile after mile.

The bored are boring and soon go to sleep,

and hours later still not a peep.

Directions are given which most ignore,

Still, there's a few that look for a door.

Feelings of movement vibrate the floor,

and under your feet, there's nothing more.

In the daylight you see the ground,

mountains, and valleys & clouds all round.

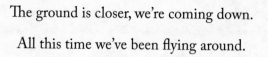

The ground is closer, we're coming down.

All this time we've been flying around.

Dove

Widely known as a symbol of peace

bringing love and serenity to us each,

even a dove can be a bird of prey,

especially to the insect that gets in its way

or to the thing that threatens its child,

then it can be extremely wild.

As parental instincts kick into gear,

rage quickly erupts to instill fear

to whatever comes into its sight

as this peaceful dove is ready to fight.

Then back to the bird widely known,

with an olive branch, so we are shown

we do what we have to do, to pass the test,

peace and love will conquer the rest.

Nap

Occasionally something comes to mind

when I stop, intending to unwind.

There is so much inside my head.

"Please relax, brain," is what I've said.

Then I clear myself of all thought,

begin at the end where I ought.

Concentrate on relaxing my toes,

slowly work up to relaxing my nose.

Then of course I get to my brain.

Stop and rest before you go insane

in order that I may nap a while

and awaken with a brand-new smile.

I really could use some rest,

so I can operate at my best.

Something should get out of my mind,

so that I can recoup while I unwind.

No Regret

Today is a day of no regret,

contemplating what's not done yet.

For, if we are still able to contemplate,

then maybe we have not left it too late.

If we still have the energy and the time,

we can stop dreaming and earn the dime

to make living our lives really great,

and I am here to say please do not wait.

Retirement is known to be wasted on the old

when the body and mind begin to mold.

Get up, do something not done before,

something hidden inside your core.

Even if only to smile at a stranger,

go ahead and laugh at the danger

and just kick your butt in gear.

Live your life without any fear.

Contemplate what is not done yet,

Make this a day of no regret...

Life's Hourglass

Whenever I take an intensely long look

at the sands of the past like an open book,

diverse emotions grab ahold of me.

From sublimely happy to very sad, I see.

Memories are nice and comfort is giving,

they help to remind me that life is for living.

So I close that book as carefully as I can

to preserve the memories in my hourglass sand.

Great choices it's true, I have multiples of.

I can fill my hourglass with sands of love.

Maybe fill it with old sands of times long past,

that good or bad went too darn fast.

Or maybe the sands of the here and now

will help me to make a brand-new vow

to do everything that I can to ensure

I live in the present, looking at the future,

helping the world to be a better place,

contributing to the life of an angelic face.

Eliminating some of the stress of their day,

not allowing their future to silently slip away,

donating to the sands in their open book.

So when they take an intensely long look,

the memories in their book of hourglass sand

have been preserved the best that I can.

They show that I cared as much as I should

and that I did all that I possibly could

to save the sands of love and tried not to destroy,

but to fill their life's hourglass with sands of joy.

Happy

Sometimes happy bubbles up to overflow.

Everyone sees it everywhere that you go.

Body language and those smiling eyes

cannot be hidden, and they tell no lies.

Even when grief has rocked your world,

a time comes when inner joy is unfurled.

Acceptance grows so that it will override

and bring a peace that you cannot hide,

one day reawakening your heart.

Joy taking you to a brand-new start

that will gently help you come to realize

you need to listen to the words of the wise

when they let you know that you will be okay.

You will smile again and have a happy day.

Then one at a time good days will multiply.

You'll wake one morning without the sigh,

looking forward to time for you to arise

and lo and behold to your surprise,

your happy will bubble up to overflow.

You will see it everywhere that you go.

Simple Pleasure

A BLT on homemade bread,

a new book you haven't read,

a butterfly in the midst of flight,

a full moon in a starry night,

life's simple pleasures

are wonderful treasures.

Embrace and cherish them all.

A happy child's shining face,

a loving and warm embrace,

picnicking on a sunshiny day

thunder crashing from far away

no matter their measure

you enjoy them at leisure.

Embrace and cherish them all.

A walk on a beach of white sand,

a parade with a marching band,

the taste of a chocolaty treat,

a word in a song and the beat,

life's simple pleasures,

are wonderful treasures.

Embrace and cherish them all.

A white cloud slowly floating by,

the smell of a freshly baked pie,

the feel of a crisp, clean sheet,

the handshake of a friend we meet,

no matter their measure,

you enjoy them at leisure.

Embrace and cherish them all.

The sounds of nature in the air,

mourning doves, for life a pair,

a phone call just to say hello,

a memory for wherever you go,

life's simple pleasures

are wonderful treasures.

Embrace and cherish them all.

Pay Attention

Frustration erupts at very miniscule things

until we realize the hurt that it brings.

Volcanic eruptions of the heated kind

never solve anything, is what I find

to be a real truth in its infinite form

as temper carries us beyond the norm.

Take time to think before making a choice

and giving our inner volcano a voice.

Volcanic ash makes it hard to breathe,

and there are words that make us seethe

with the vocabulary that anger can bring

so that I'm sorry can't fix everything.

Ensure in this life you make no mistake

by choosing the fiery wrong road to take.

Listen to the messages sent by our Lord

bringing it all to fight Satan's sword.

Say a prayer and give lots of thought

and then proceed with what you ought

to have done from the very start,

pay attention to the love in your heart.

Choices

Do not miss out on something that could be great

just because it may be hard.

Most things in life that have immense rewards

are not as easy as flipping a card.

The wonderful things we encounter are cherished

more when we work to achieve,

so the satisfaction earned making our goal

helps contribute to what we believe.

Fear is a normal problem in life's reason for

missing out on something good,

for looking life's new things straight in the eye

and doing what we should.

Do not miss out on potential; it is okay to be afraid,

we all have fears to face.

We defeat our fears with God's will, His way,

His time, and His grace.

This could be deemed as a prayer-filled task

listening to our inner voices.

We are never alone, just need to ask for His help

when we make difficult choices.

Karen Cerio

Who Are You?

Who are you when there is no one else around,

only you to keep your feet on the ground?

We try to say, "What you see is what you get,"

but our deep inside hasn't been let loose yet.

No matter the person, stranger, family, or friend,

role-playing comes natural, a means to the end.

We can be child, parent, sibling, or spouse.

It depends on what's going on inside our house,

or at church, at work, or even at play,

we are not the same person the entire day.

We can comfort a friend and say it's all right,

then turn on the person, looking for a fight.

At times many people we all have to be.

We think no one knows the real you and me,

but reality cannot be hidden by gal or lad,

God knows it all, the good and the bad.

So whoever you are and whatever you do,

when alone check deep inside for the real you.

Whoever you find when there's no one else around,

it is up to you to keep your feet on the ground.

Music

Jump-start your heart and your day.

Put on some music and let it play.

Open your eyes, your heart, and your mind.

Play music you like of any kind.

A song with rhythm, that's got a good beat,

helps you wake up and tap your feet.

Get it going, move your groove thing.

Enjoy the feelings music will bring.

You can play Beethoven and Bach,

or maybe some heavy metal rock.

How about country, old style or new?

Maybe it's doo-wop that gets to you,

or opera, with a star singing higher,

like heaven's angel, gospel choir.

Feel-good music you can turn up loud,

pretend you are singing to a crowd.

Whatever style that makes you sing,

joy and comfort it will surely bring.

Jump-start your heart and your day.

Put on some music and let it play.

Urge

I cannot think of a thing to write.

My brain has left me for tonight.

You know, it does that sometimes,

then I just cannot make rhymes

or even think of what to write about

so I merely sit down and doubt,

until such a time when ideas explode

giving me the whole mother lode

of words so I can, with pen and paper,

write until the fire is out on the taper.

Once again my brain has left for the night

so I lose the urge and no longer write.